☾

*Welcome to your Walking Stick Press guided
journal. Within these pages you'll find:*

✶

instruction to guide you on your way

✶

writing prompts to lead you to your goal

✶

blank pages to record your responses to the
prompts—to map your insights as you heal, grow,
and explore

✶

quotes to inspire, provoke, and refresh you

✶

*Along the way, feel free to jot in the margins,
add your own quotes,
let writing take you down a trail you didn't expect.
Enjoy the journey.*

✶

From *Dreams* *to* Discovery

a guided journal

Joan Mazza

Walking Stick Press

Cincinnati, Ohio

Visit our Web site at www.writersdigest.com for information on more resources for writers.

ISBN 1-58297-012-2

Edited by Michelle Howry and Jessica Yerega
Cover and interior designed by Matthew S. Gaynor
Cover photography © Red/Blue; Photonica
Production coordinated by Mark Griffin

Dedication

For my dreamgroup

About the Author

Joan Mazza, M.S. LMHC, is the author of *Dreaming Your Real Self: A Personal Approach to Dream Interpretation* (Perigee, July 1998), and *Dream Back Your Life: Transforming Your Dream Messages Into Life Action* (Perigee, July 2000). She is a psychotherapist and licensed mental health counselor with a master's degree in counseling psychology. She conducts ongoing groups in South Florida as well as national seminars on a variety of topics including:

* Journal Writing and Creativity
* Journal Writing as Self-Therapy
* Understanding Dreams and Nightmares
* How to Say No With a Smile: Setting Personal Boundaries
* When Life Gives You Lemons ...
* Creating Personal Rituals and Ceremonies
* Knowing Your Shadow and Subpersonalities
* Conscious Sexuality
* Motivate Yourself!
* Malleable Minds

As a speaker, Joan Mazza brings seminars to both professionals and the public, addressing the concerns and frustrations of people in "mid-life" crises, regardless of age. With humor and personal anecdotes, she invites people to be themselves, take risks, and dream back their lives.

She is a past-president of The Book Group of South Florida, an organization of authors and book industry professionals. Her short stories, articles, poetry, and essays have appeared in many publications, including *Playgirl*, *Personal Journaling*, and *Möbius*.

Check out her website at **www.joanmazza.com**

Table of Contents

Introduction

Deep into that darkness peering,
long I stood there, wondering,
fearing, doubting, dreaming dreams
no mortal ever dared to dream
before.

Edgar Allan Poe

Everyone dreams. At night, while we sleep, our minds are nearly as active as when we are awake. We dream throughout the night, in cycles of about ninety minutes, with each dreaming period increasing in length. These images, feelings, stories, and strange combinations of characters and places have meanings that we can decipher—if we take the time to understand their language. By dreaming, we finish the unfinished business of our day, resolve our conflicted emotions, soothe our worries, encourage ourselves, and make peace with ourselves and with others.

Dreams are hard to remember and even harder to understand. In our dreams, we seem to have wisdom and knowledge that escape us in our conscious, waking lives. When we remember and understand our dreams, we have access to this personal well of wisdom and insight. One way to gain access is by writing dreams in a daily journal.

Keeping a dream journal is more than simply recording your dreams. To get the most value out of a dream, we must know why we tell ourselves these bizarre stories with weird images, characters, and combinations of places. Then we can use this information in our lives—to make changes, choices, and decisions with good judgment and clear intention.

From Dreams to Discovery is a dream journal with specific questions and writing prompts to help any dreamer understand the messages that dreams offer. This upbeat, easy-to-follow format assists you in decoding the mysterious language of dreams and reminds you that all dreams offer important and helpful information. Beyond the superficial layer of obvious meaning, all dreams present new ways of looking at our lives, ourselves, and others. *From Dreams to Discovery* puts dreams into action.

A dream journal

A daily journal is an opportunity for reflection on our lives. It provides us a place to organize our thoughts and feelings, a way to settle down, to sort out our concerns and frustrations. It is a venue for planning our days and our lives, a space for evaluating our place in the world and the legacy we wish to leave.

In dreams, we also review and assess the events of our lives and our reactions to them. We measure ourselves against our ideal identity. Because dreaming helps us to integrate the disparate parts of ourselves to make us more whole, journaling our dreams can facilitate this natural process.

You may choose to write at a computer or longhand in a beautiful bound book, with colored pencils or pens, making drawings or not. If you write regularly—preferably every day, even if it's only for a few minutes—the enormous value of this small effort will soon become clear.

By journaling your dreams in a systematic and organized way, you will recognize the metaphors and symbols in your dreams. A pattern revealed by a series of dreams will likely reveal a similar pattern in your life. These connections and associations to waking concerns and problems can help point the way toward health and wholeness. They reveal the many layers of dream meanings.

Through dreams, we tell ourselves when to be more courageous and more honest, when to change our attitude and take better care of ourselves. By writing down the dreams and reflecting on their content, by answering the provocative questions suggested here, we can decipher many possible meanings. This inner work can help us reach a higher level of self-awareness, including confidence and trust in our own minds.

A dream journal makes a fruitful intersection of two reflective paths—dreamwork and journal writing—facilitating self-awareness and insight. *From Dreams to Discovery* teaches you how to combine the techniques of dreamwork and journal writing to understand your dreams and understand yourself.

Some people regard discipline as a chore. For me, it is a kind of order that sets me free to fly.

Julie Andrews

chapter 1

Getting Started

Just keep going. Everybody gets
better if they keep at it.

Ted Williams

There are many ways to understand and interpret dreams. This book
offers a variety of techniques to help you understand your own
dreams by journaling about them. The way you see the world
and make meaning of it will influence how you interpret your
own dreams. If you take a spiritual or religious view of your
life, then you will interpret your dreams in light of this viewpoint. If your approach is practical or scientific, then your interpretations will likely be more in terms of pragmatic
applications, rather than philosophical explorations. However,
it is possible to approach dreams from multiple viewpoints and
thereby benefit from the multiple layers of wisdom that
dreams offer.

How to use this book

Each chapter discusses a particular way one might look at a
dream. Because there are many different points of entry to possible dream meanings, I have called them *doorways*. You can
take a particular dream and allow yourself to choose a doorway
based on what feels right in the moment. Because dreams are
not linear, you can begin exploring them through any doorway

first, knowing that entering the other doorways will get simpler and more sensible as you continue. Think of the dream discovery process as a journey down a hallway. All the doorways lead to different rooms, but they are all part of the same structure.

At the end of a brief description of the doorway, you will find writing prompts to explore the meaning and significance of your dream. Each section can be used as a doorway to understanding any individual dream. All dreams are meaningful on multiple levels and may speak to several different areas of your life simultaneously, so going through several doorways will yield more meanings.

A single "big" dream with vivid imagery and strong emotions can be examined through all the sections (doorways) of the book to find many layers of meaning.

See the dream worksheet on page 19. You may want to make additional copies of this worksheet to record many dreams. By using the dream worksheet, you will have a ready way to capture the most important aspects of a dream before they fade from memory, as they so quickly do.

Why keep a dream journal?

Journals provide a safe place for us to ventilate our most personal concerns, fears, hopes, and desires. It is the one place where we can be totally open and honest with ourselves, without fear of judgment, rejection, or criticism. We can complain and be as inappropriate and immature as we like, in ways we would never allow ourselves to be publicly. In our own time and style, we can reflect on what we have written and see it in a larger perspective. In some ways, a dream journal is better than going to a therapist. It allows us make our own discoveries about the meaning of our dreams at our own pace. Our dreams give us regular status reports on our inner lives. By journaling dreams, we can find our way to our own truths at the pace and with the methods that we find most comfortable.

At the end of a brief description of the doorway, you will find writing prompts to explore the meaning and significance of your dream.

> By journaling dreams, we
> can find our way to our
> own truths...

Benefits of a dream journal

Keeping a dream journal provides many benefits.

* ★ *Provides a safe place to ventilate thoughts and feelings.* Because we can't always say what we feel or think, a journal provides a place for us to do this without fear of consequences. We can be totally honest and not worry about our image to others. A dream journal *allows us to speak our truth.*

* ★ *Prepares a framework to examine dreams, especially those that are embarrassing or frightening.* Dream content is sometimes offensive, even to the dreamer. The journal is a place for looking at those aspects of dreams that are hard to face.

* ★ *Offers an opportunity to examine emotions and to reflect on the day's events.* Because we are so busy, it's hard to find reflective time to consider our lives. Keeping a journal allows us to do this.

* ★ *Turns the confusing content of the dream into a meaningful story.* By writing them down, we turn the jumbled thoughts, images, and feelings in our dreams into something we can examine and understand.

* ★ *Gives us a sense of perspective.* Immersed in our problems of the moment, we can sometimes lose sight of the whole picture of our lives. Keeping a journal helps us see this larger perspective—things change and we grow; nothing stays the same.

* ★ *Prepares a record of dream (and waking) patterns and concerns.* Having a written record of our dreams and our concerns makes it easier for us to discern patterns, habits, and familiar obstacles, helping us to move beyond these stuck places.

* ★ *Forces us to listen to ourselves and our dreams.* By keeping a dream journal, we are listening to our own voices, thoughts, and feelings—our psyche's attempts to find solutions. Without it, we are unlikely to focus enough to

listen to ourselves.

* *Helps organize our thinking.* A journal, by its very nature, assists us in clarifying questions in our minds and organizing separate issues and feelings. Writing down our thoughts in sentences and paragraphs helps us to organize our ideas. Otherwise, they are likely to rattle around in our heads, causing us to feel distressed and overwhelmed.

* *Allows us to be socially inappropriate.* In most circumstances, adults are not supposed to throw a tantrum, fall apart, or celebrate our grandiosity. The journal allows us to say anything we want. It grants us permission to fantasize about lust, revenge, recklessness, and standing ovations.

* *Shines a light on our dark side, our Shadow.* We all have aspects of ourselves we don't want to show the world. A dream journal mines these places we think of as shameful—and often reveals positive, hidden energy and creativity.

* *Puts a new spin on our problems.* When we listen to our dreams, we are able to hear other ways to evaluate our problems. We see solutions we hadn't thought of before.

* *Raises consciousness and self-awareness.* Dreams remind us of how we play a part in everything that happens to us, even if it is only in our interpretation of events that we can't control (like the weather). We become aware of our role in our own happiness and unhappiness, as well as our impact on others.

* *Captures our moments of greatness.* Most of us are so busy being critical of ourselves and noticing our mistakes that we miss our successes and triumphs. Keeping a journal gives us a place to notice these shining moments and celebrate them.

* *Illuminates our authentic self.* We all have parts of ourselves that are submerged by the tasks and responsibili-

ties of our everyday lives. We often put aside our true feelings, hopes, and desires, concentrating instead on what we believe is a higher priority at the moment. A dream journal shines a light on these authentic aspects of ourselves.

★ *Answers questions about our life and choices.* Dreams offer insights we can take into action in our lives. Paying attention to these messages can relieve us of some of our ordinary confusion.

★ *Offers ideas for future creative projects.* These projects can include stories, essays, poems, books, articles, paintings, sculpture, dance, music, etc. Dreams and creativity come from the same place. By paying attention to dreams, you will discover a vast well of creative inspiration.

Dream dictionaries

Because all symbols have private, personal meanings, dream dictionaries are usually not very helpful in understanding the symbols. However, you can create your own dream dictionary by writing down your frequently used symbols and what you discover they mean *to you*. When the symbol appears in a dream again, you can remind yourself of what it meant to you the last time. However, our use of symbols changes with our emotional and psychological needs.

Basic steps for dreamwork

Beginning anything new may seem daunting at first. How do you begin to keep a dream journal? Below are step-by-step instructions. These will help decipher the layers of meaning in your dreams. But remember, these are only suggestions. As you explore your dreams, you will discover what methods and strategies work best for you. You will improve your recall and understand your dreams more quickly. From those insights about yourself and how you are functioning, you will be able to take positive action in your life.

1. Expect to understand at least one layer of your dream's meaning.

2. Imagine yourself waking and recording the dream.

3. Keep this dream journal at your bedside.

4. Record your dream on the dream worksheet (see page 19).

5. Make note of all details in the dream—especially the weird ones.

6. Focus on your emotions—particularly those that are strong or disturbing.

7. Give the dream a title that captures its specific content. (*Hiding from the bear* is a better title than *A big animal chases me* because it is more explicit.)

8. Reflect on your own interpretations and understanding of the dream.

9. Choose the method(s) of dreamwork for your journal that seem to suit your dream best. Or, take one very vivid dream, nightmare, or recurrent dream that has seized your attention. Use that dream to go through all the sections of this book.

10. When discussing your dreams with others, remember that dreams are very personal. You and only you are the final authority on their meaning and significance in your life.

11. Take the insights of the dream into action in your life.

Immersed in our problems of the moment, we can sometimes lose sight of the whole picture of our lives. Keeping a journal helps us see this larger perspective— things change and we grow; nothing stays the same.

Recording methods

The best method of recording dreams is the one that works best for you. Some people keep a notebook or pad at their bedside. Others prefer to use a voice-activated tape recorder to catch dreams, and they transcribe the dreams later when they are more awake.

The worksheet on page 19 is for recording dreams—even fragments of dreams, which can offer important information. As soon as you remember a dream, fill out as much of the form as you can. Any part of it, like any of the doorways, can reveal a layer of meaning.

As you become more experienced, consider changing the worksheet to suit your style and preferred way of working.

Digging deeper

Dreams can be interpreted on several layers, both literally and metaphorically. An interpretation that resonates with the dreamer on one layer is only one of many possible interpretations. Each dream will capture concerns in several areas of the dreamer's life, though one may stand out more than the rest.

Most dreamers hear the literal layer of a dream's meaning readily. For example, you might dream about taking a trip right after buying a plane ticket. You may believe that you fully understand the dream by making this connection. But dreams can have many meanings for different aspects of life. These multilayered meanings are usually found in the dream in metaphorical and symbolic language. A trip or journey in your dream refers to more than the planned vacation. It may also be about your life journey, your career path, or your relationship journey with someone significant.

Each section of this book suggests a different way to enter a dream, though all of them may be used with a dream that has been a longtime puzzle or of considerable concern.

Think of each section as a doorway to enter your dream's meanings. With every dream, think about the questions below before proceeding through the doorways.

1. What is the obvious meaning of the dream? What literal meaning makes sense? (If your driving is out of control in your dream, might this be a warning that you need to literally drive more carefully?)

2. Beyond the *literal* meaning, how is the dream a *metaphor* of your life? (In what way are you out of control in your life? Do you need to put on the brakes in some way?)

Date and approximate time of dream:

Title:

Dream contents:

Dream story (in three sentences):

Dream ending:

Emotions of the dream:

Vivid images:

Waking events of the day before the dream, including problems, concerns, focus:

Connections, interpretations:

Main message or moral of the dream:

Literal and metaphoric meanings:

General information on remembering dreams

Forgetting your dreams is normal. Because we dream every night—as many as five to seven times a night—it is clear that all of us forget the dreams we have. If you are one of the big re-callers, waking up with a memory of two or three dreams on several mornings a week, you are still recalling only a small fraction of the dreams you have.

> Most of us forget our dreams because we're too busy to take the time to remember.

Most of us forget our dreams because we're too busy to take the time to remember. Remembering dreams, however, is a skill that can be learned. Since we all have thousands of dreams each year, remembering them and doing dreamwork with all of them would be impossible. But perhaps you'd like to be better than normal, remembering some of your dreams and understanding the meaning and significance of at least some of those you remember.

Forgetting dreams does not mean you're afraid to re-member them or that you are repressing them. If you want to remember more dreams, it will take effort and attention, but it is not complicated. Follow the steps below for several nights in a row and you, too, can be someone with many dreams when you wake up. Then you will have to choose which ones you want to record and select for dreamwork.

Tips for remembering your dreams

1. Expect to remember your dreams.
2. Before going to sleep, imagine yourself waking and recording the dream.
3. Keep your dream journal at your bedside with a pen or pencil, preferably one that you particularly like. (You can purchase a pen with a light at the tip.)
4. Avoid using alarm clocks to wake yourself. If you must use them on workdays, select a free day for remember-ing dreams and allow yourself to awaken naturally. On the days when you can go back to sleep for an extra hour

or more of rest, you are most likely to catch a dream when you wake up.

5. Upon waking, you probably rolled over. Return your body to its most comfortable sleeping position. (Many people say they remember more dreams when they sleep on their backs.)

6. Stay in bed for a few minutes and review the dream scenes and sequences in your mind. Memorize them without trying to analyze or understand them.

7. Write down whatever you remember in as much detail as you can. If you are pressed for time and can only make notes, record the most unusual images and the strongest emotions to capture the essence of the dream before it evaporates. (If you record nothing at this time, you will most likely have nothing to recall later when you want to. Dreams seem to retreat to that mysterious realm from which they came!)

8. Even a dream fragment is often packed with meaning. Fragments have the brevity and precision that comes with simplicity and are well worth exploring. No dream is too short. (For example, an image of flying clocks might be showing you that you are feeling anxious about your life going by too quickly. Time flies!)

9. If you don't remember any dreams, write down your feelings when you get up—your emotions (sad, anxious, happy, playful, worried, eager) and your body state (energetic, logy, stiff, agile, achy, agitated). Or you can write something about the issue in your life that seems most on your mind.

10. Notice *when* you remember dreams. You will find you have greater recall in certain situations, such as when you are on vacation, in unfamiliar beds, when you go back to sleep on a day off, or after a nap. Once you determine your best times to recall dreams, take advantage

> Your ability to understand
> the meaning in your dreams
> will improve with practice.

of them when they present themselves, or create these situations more often.

11. Drink a lot of water at bedtime, and you will be more likely to interrupt your dreaming cycle, thereby remembering one you might have otherwise missed. (However, this method is not recommended for the elderly.)

12. If you catch a dream in the middle of the night when you get up for a drink of water or to use the bathroom, make a quick note (as suggested in #7) to capture the dream. Then record it in full in the morning. A few words can often unlock a previously "forgotten" dream. Then choose a doorway to learn more.

If you repeat these steps regularly, you will remember dreams. When you have too many dreams to deal with, choose those that are most vivid and emotionally powerful to examine in detail. Your ability to understand the meaning in your dreams will improve with practice.

Ask yourself a specific question

Remember that before going to sleep, you can ask a question to get an answer to a problem in your life. This idea of consciously focusing the dream's content is called *incubating a dream* or *programming a dream*. By writing the question down, you are activating your unconscious to work on this concern while you sleep, as well as while you are awake. You'll get an answer to your question in your dream. This also facilitates recalling dreams—your question and the expectation of an answer primes you to remember, even if it's only a dream fragment. Fragments—even skimpy ones—can be rich with metaphorical meanings, just like a good poem.

Use personal memory tricks that work for you

When you desire to do something new, drawing on a method that *already works for you* is a good beginning. In your daily life, you often have to make a mental note of something to do at another time. In a conversation, you may want to ask the person a question, but don't want to interrupt. So you "flag" that thought for a later time when you can ask.

Consider how your usual tricks to remember something can help you in remembering your dreams. Knowing your own tricks for remembering something will provide a method to remember more dreams. For example, try telling yourself that you will remember your dream when you pick up your toothbrush in the morning or see your dream journal on your night table. If you regularly remember dreams when you are taking a shower, imagine that moment of remembering when you go to bed at night. Go with what works for you!

Prompts

Choose the prompts that interest you most, and use the blank pages that follow to record your responses.

one

What methods do you use to remember to do something?

★ Try lists, mental pictures, rhyming sounds in your head, leaving an item conspicuously in your view (so you'll remember to take it with you), sticky notes on your front door or dashboard of the car, etc. Translate these methods into a way to remember dreams. People often remember dreams while they are driving. Perhaps you can place a sticky note on your dashboard that says, "What did you dream?"

two

For the times when you *do* remember a dream, how and when does that happen? Can you help create more of those times?

three

If you remembered your dreams regularly, when and how would you remember? Describe this in detail below. What would you do? Where would you be? What would you be doing as you remembered the dream? (Lying in bed? Resting on the couch? Standing in the shower? Driving your car? Riding a bus or train? Drinking coffee?)

four

Write down your dream-remembering process.

Dreaming permits each
and every one of us to
be quietly and safely
insane every night of
our lives.

Charles W. Dement

Dreams—A microscope through which we look at the hidden occurrences in our soul.

Erich Fromm

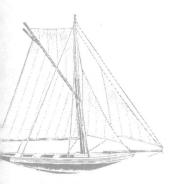

How can you be certain
that your whole life is
not a dream?

Descartes

chapter 2

Doorway of Dream Emotions:
strong feelings for strong meanings

The past is not dead; it is not even past. People live on inner time; the moment in which a decisive thought or feeling takes place can be at any time. Timeless feelings are common to all of us.

Martha Graham

One of the most direct routes to understanding dream meanings is to capture the feelings you have in your dream. Your feelings in the dream may be very different from those you have after waking from the dream. During the dream experience, you might feel sexually aroused or angry, but when you wake up you might be appalled at the actions you took in the dream. Conversely, you may do something wonderful and fantastic in a dream, such as fly, and feel elated at your spectacular performance. When you wake, you might be surprised at your dream achievement. These emotional contrasts might point the way toward overcoming a fear of doing something in waking life.

Dominant emotion in the dream

The strongest emotion in your dream is often the key to the dream's meaning, which is why this is the first doorway we will explore.

That powerful emotion from the dream often echoes and exaggerates something left unfinished—emotionally and psychologically—from the day preceding the dream. If your boss ignores what you say at a meeting, you might dream older siblings have left you out of their party or abandoned you in a dangerous place. Your dream creation is an effort to resolve this emotional state and restore you to a psychological balance. Frequently, we have emotions that we are unable to acknowledge, honor, or express during the day because we feel it is unsafe. If we say what we really think and feel, we might be fired from our jobs!

Unexpressed emotions often come through in a dream, perhaps in an exaggerated form—the way a caricature of someone exaggerates certain features. If you are feeling put down or dismissed by someone's social slight, you might intellectually know that the person didn't mean harm or was preoccupied, but you may still feel hurt or rejected. In your dream, your hurt might be exaggerated to mortal wounding.

Capturing the strong emotions of a dream is an excellent entrance to dreamwork. You might think of it as the main doorway. Keep in mind that we are more likely to remember dreams with strong negative emotions than those dreams that are pleasant.

Some emotions that appear in dreams are:

Joy
Worry
Anxiety
Sadness
Interest
Grief

Bliss

Despair

Excitement

Fear

Curiosity

Delight

Terror

Sexual arousal/interest

Pleasure

Emotions can change during your dream

Many dreams have an evolution of emotional states in the course of the dream. Often, a dream will start in neutral emotional territory, with the dreamer feeling bland or unemotional. As the dream progresses, a mounting fear or anxiety may develop, or the dreamer might proceed from curiosity to intense frustration or sexual desire. Noting the evolution of emotions during the dream may help you see what daytime issues this dream is addressing.

For example, you might dream you are walking in a park, feeling content, and then become worried about being followed. Then you are certain a dangerous person is trailing you. From there, you become terrified and run for your life. The feelings change from neutral (or pleasant) to scary. This common dream might be asking you to examine how things look good at first, but then get dangerous or out of control in some way. The dream might be addressing your carefree attitude that prevents you from being cautious or prepared. On the other hand, it might be saying that you worry about non-existent dangers, preventing you from enjoying life. Only you, the dreamer, will know whether the dream is a criticism of what you already do or a suggestion to see things differently.

Emotions after you wake

Look at your emotional reaction to your dream *after* you wake. How do those emotions differ from those you had during the dream? It is quite common to have a dream of doing something or experiencing some event, and then reacting with horror and dismay when you wake up. Perhaps you have quit smoking or drinking, but you have relapsed in the dream. Or you're in a state of terror in the dream, or of terrible grief and anguish over the loss of a loved one. You're likely to wake and think with relief, "Oh, thank goodness it's only a dream!"

This emotional contrast may tell you something in itself, though the events didn't really happen. Perhaps you are addressing a temptation (to drink, stray from your agreements with yourself or others) and the dream is warning you of how terrible you would feel if you did this behavior. If you tend to withhold your emotions, maybe the dream is telling you it's time to let them out. Dreams ask us to live more emotionally balanced lives.

> It is quite common to have a dream of doing something or experiencing some event, and then reacting with horror and dismay when you wake up.

Prompts

Choose the prompts that interest you most, and use the blank pages that follow to record your responses.

one

List the emotions in your dream. Circle the strongest emotions.

    ✶ Look at the emotions you circled. What does this tell you? Write down any interpretations that jump to mind now.

    ✶ How do these emotions mirror a waking set of circumstances or events in your life on the day before you had the dream? If I am feeling very anxious in my dream, that might reflect the anxiety I felt earlier in the day about something that the dream is trying to deal with.

    ✶ How do these emotions in the dream contrast with your waking feelings after the dream?

two

How do your emotions change during the dream? (Do they change from frightened to feeling confident? Or from feeling competent to feeling increasingly overwhelmed or out of control?)

    ✶ How does this pattern of emotion match your usual waking reaction style? (Escalating, appeasing, denying, distracting, etc.)

three

Does the evolution of your emotions in your dream tell you something about your emotional patterns in day-to-day life? (Do you start out in a relationship idealizing the other person and then move toward contempt, disrespect, and genuine dislike? Do you try to ignore situations you know are headed for disaster?)

four

What emotions do you have when reflecting on this dream after you wake?

five

How do the dream emotions feel compared to your waking emotions? The same, different, opposite, or modified in some way? Write down this comparison. (I might feel frightened in the dream, but experience the dream images as odd or humorous on waking.)

six

If your waking emotions are in contrast to those in your dream, what does this tell you?

seven

Remember the dream is a compensation for any waking emotional stance. How is it telling you to experience waking events differently?

In dreams and in love
there are no
impossibilities.

János Arany

The future belongs to
those who believe in the
beauty of their dreams.

Eleanor Roosevelt

chapter 3

Doorway of Dream Body States:
physical sensations, orientation in space

Newman's first law: It is useless to
put on your brakes when you're
upside down.

Paul Newman

Emotions are often manifested in physical as well as psychological states. We get headaches or stomachaches when we are upset. We may faint or feel nauseated when we are frightened.

In dreams, too, we may have body sensations that are ways of depicting our inner life. The metaphorical expressions of our daily speech become literal pictures in dreams.

If, in a dream, your physical sensations are unusual, this may be a metaphor for how you feel you are situated in the world. You might be *sick to death* of doing the same old thing, *sick and tired* of your job, or feel as if your world has been turned *upside down* by an illness in the family. You may be having *rough* times and express this in the literal texture of your dream surroundings.

Body orientation: up, down, or tilted

The way your body is oriented in a dream can provide clues to the meaning of the dream. Perhaps you are upside down or tilted, trying to right yourself in the dream. These might express how you feel your life or values are upside down and you need to "get right with the world." Or you might feel off-balance or off-center. These physical experiences in the dream usually capture the essence of a waking dissatisfaction or frustration. Conversely, the pleasant physical sensations associated with dreaming may show us a highly satisfied sense of ourselves that our waking modesty and humility won't let us experience fully. If life feels easy and good, you might float or feel as if you're coasting in your dreams.

Touch

Similarly, we experience other body states in our dreams, such as feeling pressure to our bodies (squeezed or squashed), or feeling our skin being scratched. We may feel kicked or pushed. These are all metaphorical expressions in our language about how people and circumstances might intrude on our choices and freedoms. *Don't push me. You're squashing my views.* They tell us we feel uncomfortable (or comfortable) with our present circumstances.

Touching a physical surface in the dream, you might find it pliable, soft, hard, or rough. A rough texture might mean you feel irritated, raw, or "rubbed the wrong way." In contrast, smooth and silky textures might be saying things feel easy.

Movement

In your dreams, you might be rocking, wandering, lifting, sliding, or slipping. For example, if you are flying, falling, or paralyzed in your dream, each of these dream states can be metaphorical ways of expressing your present situation in your waking life.

✶ The sensation of flying in your dreams is usually very pleasurable, mirroring success and satisfied feelings in your waking experience. Ask yourself how you are "flying" in your life.

✶ Falling may be a statement that you feel you have not met your own standards or expectations. You might be "falling down" on the job or in your pursuit of goals. You could also be "falling" in love.

✶ Sensations of paralysis may be metaphors to tell you how you are feeling "stuck" or "paralyzed" about making a decision.

In each case, the metaphors of body states in your dream reflects the literal rather than idiomatic meaning of the words. In dreams, we take the clichés of speech and turn them into pictorial and physical representations.

one

What do you notice about your physical orientation in your dream? Are you up? Are you down? Do you feel off-balance? Centered?

two

At what point in the dream is this awareness most intense? At the beginning? At the end of the dream? After you've woken up?

three

Does your physical orientation feel pleasant, unpleasant, or something else? Describe the sensation and your feelings about it.

four

How does this physical sensation translate into a metaphor about your life in some way? (For example, a dream about falling could mean your life is unsteady, or you're unsure of your footing/foundation. A dream about repeatedly going over the same territory could mean you're "in a rut.")

five

How does the texture of something in your dream reflect the "texture" of what it represents in your life? (Who or what is rough, hard, smooth?)

six

If you are moving or paralyzed, what does this tell you about movement or progress in your life?

seven

If the movement is a status report on your life's journey, how are you doing?

Choose the prompts that interest you most, and use the blank pages that follow to record your responses.

In a dream you are never 47
eighty.

Anne Sexton

Dreams are real while
they are happening.
Can we say any more
about life?

Havelock Ellis

50 |

Our dreams drench us in
senses, and senses steep us
again in dream.

Amos Bronson Alcott

chapter 4

Doorway of Dream Language:
metaphors, clichés, and favorite expressions

Language is the picture and
counterpart of thought.

Mark Hopkins

In the previous doorway of dream body states, we got a glimpse of
how language—particularly our own personal use of expressions—can show up as literal images or actions in dreams. All
speech is symbolic. Many words have more than one meaning.
For different people, the same word will carry a different emotional charge. Even ordinary words have different values to different people. Saying *baby* to one person brings up warm,
nurturing, or protective feelings. To someone who has not been
able to conceive children she wanted, the word might trigger
feelings of disappointment and loss. One person can be of-
fended by a word; another delights at its bluntness. In dreams,
we look beyond the denotations in the dictionary and even beyond connotations in common usage. Dreamwork reveals our

innermost concerns and feelings; we must uncover our own personal meanings to words and symbols.

Symbols and metaphors

We dream in the language of symbols and metaphors, just as we use them in speech. We can more easily understand our dreams when we recognize our *patterns* of speech and thought. For example, a person who works with mechanical things, such as an engineer or inventor, might say that things are "running smoothly," or that they are "falling to pieces" or "breaking down." He might say someone has a "screw loose" or needs a "tune-up." Similar imagery and metaphors will show up in dreams. At times of stress in his relationship, he might see himself in a dream, trying repeatedly to fix something, but unable to get it to work. Or perhaps he can't find the right part. Something is missing! As a dreamworker, I would ask him, "What's like that in your life? What's missing? What can't you get to work properly?"

Tuning into your own language (another metaphor!) in this way will help you to work with your dreams in a dream journal.

Puns, double meanings, and word play

Look for puns and double meanings in your dreams. Sometimes we don't notice these until we say the dream aloud or write it down. After writing a dream down, see what double meanings might be there. In one of my dreams, a writer friend had moved to a house with a curtain at the entrance instead of a door with a lock. I wondered why she wasn't worried that her cat would get out. I realized my dream was really about *my* concern about unintentionally letting the cat out of the bag—about revealing too much in my own writing.

If someone trips over a pail in your dream, you might be playing off the expression, "kick the bucket." If you dream that you've stabbed someone—especially if you feel no remorse or horror at this act—what does this person do that you might like to attempt, or "take a stab at"? If you feel you're "up the creek without a paddle," your dream might show you that emotion in pictures.

Foreign words and expressions

Many of us have adopted expressions and curses in languages other than our native tongue. Some words in the slang of other cultures capture our emotions better than any words in American English. I grew up in New York, of Sicilian descent, in a mixed neighborhood of predominantly Italians and Jews. Expressions in Yiddish and Sicilian have stayed with me as choice words when I need them. Words like *puttanà, chutzpah,* and *shmuck* have powerful emotional associations. They remind me, both positively and negatively, of my origins, my youth, and my childhood hopes and fantasies. Hearing them in a dream can trigger memories related to the message of the dream.

If you have unusual or foreign words in your dreams, you might consider where they come from and what they mean to you personally, beyond the definition you would find in a book. You will likely associate them with certain people or particular emotional states. In addition, a character who seems strange or foreign or who uses these words may be a symbol for the whole culture. This figure may embody whatever stereotypes your less-than-politically-correct unconscious assigns to the group.

Your favorite expressions and clichés

Notice your own favorite expressions for feelings, especially when you're angry or frustrated. Your journal is a good place to discover how you describe your emotions. My words to describe feeling stressed out frequently contain metaphors about breath and water. I say I feel as if I'm "too busy to catch my breath" and that I'm "suffocating or drowning in chores and paperwork." These expressions manifest themselves in my dreams through images of being in water and unable to come up for air, or being swamped by tidal waves, or being afraid of flooding.

If you're not sure what some of your favorite expressions are, ask someone who knows you well. These will show up in your dreams, accounting, in part, for your repeated use of certain dream images and dream themes.

Prompts

Choose the prompts that interest you most, and use the blank pages that follow to record your responses.

one

What puns and double entendres appear in your dreams? Look for them after you record your dream on the worksheet.

two

What expressions do you use often? Make a list.

three

Ask a friend who knows you well to tell you the expressions you use a lot. List them. Use this to open a discussion of what your friend has observed about you that you don't know about yourself.

four

Look at your daily tasks and jobs. If these were translated into metaphors, what might you say? (*I'm really cooking. I'm in over my head at work. This is child's play. My life needs a chiropractic adjustment. I need to sow some healthier seeds.*) Have some fun and try your own here.

five

When you dislike someone, what words are you likely to use? (*Drip, schmuck, ditz, loony, low-life, snake*) Make a list and re-member that this is not a time to be politically correct. This is a personal journal, after all. Do these favorite slurs show up as images in dreams? How?

six

What positive words do you use as pet names and expressions of affection? (*You're a peach!*) List them.

seven

Make note of your dream puns and list them. (A man dreams of webs and spiders, both of which he dislikes and fears. But he also creates Web sites for the Internet, and both words are part of his professional vocabulary.)

⭐ When you look for puns, what other layers of meaning do you hear?

eight

Do you swear? Your choice of words may tell you something about the strength of your feelings as well as a particular quality to them. (If I say I've been *screwed over*, that's very different from saying that someone *got under my skin*. The difference in the metaphors may be more than a difference in meaning.) List your favorite curses.

nine

When you are feeling very stressed out, how do you describe it? (*Drowning, suffocating, fainting, numb, paralyzed*)

* When you're very afraid? (*Quaking, shaking, wanting to disappear*)

* When you're extremely happy or contented? (*A pig in mud, a duck in a fish pond, jumping for joy*)

* When you're angry? (*Seeing red, exploding, flying off the handle, bouncing off the walls*)

* Do these metaphors show up as literal images in your dreams? Describe one.

ten

How do you talk about your feelings?

* If talking about your feelings is difficult for you, do you have some means for putting a lid on them? (*Taking a shower, going for a walk, exercising, eating*) Note: If you do any of these activities in your dreams, that behavior might reflect that you are trying to deny or suppress an emotion that is difficult for you to honor when you are awake.

Language, as symbol, determines much of the nature and quality of our experience.

Sonia Johnson

60 | It takes a person who is
wide awake to make his
dreams come true.

Roger Ward Babson

62 | Dreams are the
touchstones of our
character.

Henry David Thoreau

chapter 5

Doorway of Dream Characters:
people, animals, and unknown figures

My characters never die screaming in
rage. They attempt to pull themselves
back together and go on. And that's
basically a conservative view of life.

Jane Smiley

We cast the characters in our dream, costume them, and decide what
they will say and do. We make these choices unconsciously, but
purposefully. Every person in our dreams is there for a reason.
We put them all there and we wrote the script.

Familiar faces in your dreams
Each character in your dream can be interpreted in several
ways, based on your associations, feelings, and thoughts
about the character, their actions in the dream, and your reactions on waking. You may see the character as a part of you
as well as a real person in your life. Both layers, self and other

usually have meaning. That is, if I dream of my close friend, Joyce Sweeney, my dream may address whatever rough edges I have with her at the time of the dream. She may also be a symbol for all my sisterly feelings, or stand for my feelings about women generally. Because she is also an author and my writing mentor, she is a symbol for the fiction writer. In that sense, in some dreams, she represents the fiction writer part of me. Each of these perspectives will offer different dream meanings, and each may be "correct" on its own level.

Strangers in your dreams

Strangers and shadowy characters whose faces you don't see in your dreams are more likely to represent unknown, lost, or denied parts of yourself. By not owning up to our negative impulses, or our "Shadow," as it is sometimes called, we project these emotions onto other people both in our dreams and in our waking lives. When we cannot feel our own anger, we might project it onto others. In our dreams, we give the rage to another character.

In working with these fearful or repulsive dream figures, expect to be surprised. They often have something of value to say when we pause to listen with an open mind.

Children, pets, animals

Children are important in our lives. For some people, children are the center of their lives. Concerns for them will make their way into our dreams. We worry about them, and they need us.

Similarly, people dream of their pets because these animals are in our daily lives and are important to us. We like to give them human attributes and we have strong feelings about them. We delight when they show us they understand us.

Our pets and children can also represent parts of ourselves. My two dogs represent different aspects of my personality. Other animals or figures in dreams, including strange, composite, or alien figures, may represent totem animals, other people, or parts of us. We can understand the role of these figures by asking ourselves the same questions we did about characters we recognize.

Choose the prompts that interest you most, and use the blank pages that follow to record your responses.

one

Make a list of the characters in your dreams.

    ★ See if the list can be divided into natural categories such as: people I know, people I don't know (living or dead), famous people and celebrities, people who aren't in my life anymore, strangers, people without faces, monsters, angels, animals, and other figures who may or may not be human.

two

What current issues do you have unresolved with the people who are in your dreams?

    ★ If you don't recognize these characters as people whom you know, describe them—what are they like? What personality traits do they exemplify?

three

What do the characters do in my dreams?

    ★ How do I feel about him/her?

    ★ Who does this sound like? (This may be a description of a real person in your life or a part of you or both.)

four

Ask the above questions of people you don't know who appear in your dreams, such as celebrities. (I might describe Oprah as intelligent, responsible, compassionate, and funny. It doesn't matter what she's "really" like to someone else.) Who is like that in my life today?

five

What statement am I making about this real person? Is there something I need to say to this person? (Notice that the dream might offer both positive and negative traits, unlike our waking selves. The dream is more balanced than our waking consciousness.)

Prompts

Choose the prompts that interest you most, and use the blank pages that follow to record your responses.

six

Characters in dreams also represent parts of us. How are these characters parts of you? (Yes, even the bad, dangerous characters in your dream.)

> ✶ What is this part of you trying to communicate? How is this a lost part of yourself?
>
> ✶ How is this a part of you that is seeking your attention because you've ignored it?
>
> ✶ Begin to write a dialog with the individual characters to find out what they want and why they are in your dream.

A Sample Dialog*

> *A weird creature is in my dream. It's chasing me.*
> *I'm frightened, but I ask, "Who are you?"*
> *"I'm your stifled creativity."*
> *"What creativity?"*
> *"The one who used to draw and design clothes."*
> *"What do you want?"*
> *"Get back to your art. It will calm you."*

*Note: This exercise often brings surprising and very enlightening results. It may feel silly at first, but the wisdom spoken by these dream elements is often quite amazing. They will tell us to quit smoking, start exercising, get more sleep, and to stay away from people who mistreat us. They will even give us advice about writing and other artistic expressions.

seven

While any character in your dream may be a part of you, those characters you recognize may also be themselves. How does your dream character differ from that person in waking life?

> ✶ What new information does the dream tell you about this person?
>
> ✶ Is this information accurate? Might it be an exaggerated portrayal of something you consciously deny?
>
> ✶ What can you do to explore the possibility suggested by the dream?

★ How is this character a part of you projected onto the other person?

★ If the character is someone you recognize, but who is no longer in your life, who in your life *now* do you relate to the same way? (If I dream about my deceased mother, she may be acting as a symbol for someone in my life who is as nosy as she was.)

eight

Describe a shadowy or fearful dream figure.

★ What are its traits and habits?

★ What do you know about it without any "evidence"? (We might know in a dream that someone has a knife, even though we haven't seen it.)

★ How does your dream character express your forbidden thoughts and emotions?

★ What does the dream character have to tell you?

★ Dialog in your journal with this character. Ask it questions and write down the answers as they come to you.

nine

Describe any children who appear in your dreams.

★ How do these dream children represent parts of you?

★ How do they represent other people or concerns in your life?

ten

List any animal characters in your dreams.

★ What do you know about them from their behavior in the dream? (They are sneaking about, so they must be up to mischief!)

★ How do they represent other people or concerns in your life? (A Polar bear in my dream represents solitude, survival in face of harsh elements, and a need to hibernate. It will likely mean other things to someone else.)

Every river that I know
is dreaming of the sea.

Johnny Clegg

Only in our dreams are 73
we free. The rest of the
time we need wages.

Terry Pratchett

We are near awakening
when we dream that we
dream.

  *Baron Friedrich von
    Hardenberg*

chapter 6

Doorway of Dream Images

Tell it with pictures—direct it like you
were making a silent movie.

John Sean O'Feeny Ford

The images in our dreams are part of our creation, just as all the other elements are. Many times, these are puzzling or hard to describe. Yet when we do put them into words and pictures, we are able to make a connection that helps us to understand the meaning of the dream.

Bizarre images

Some dream images are very strange. The pieces don't seem to fit. We see people doing things we believe they would never do. Structures, places, and vehicles are built in ways that are impossible. Whatever the image, we created it to make a statement to ourselves. It isn't "simply nonsense" or it wouldn't be in our dream. The meaning of the images makes sense in the context of the dream and in the context of the events of our day preceding the dream. A dream about tearing off all the book covers in a store might be a statement about feeling judged by appearance alone. You can't judge a book by its cover!

In one woman's dream, she realized she had neglected

to feed her friend's pet rabbit. When she arrived at the cage, the rabbit had shriveled into a small lump of coal. Upon reflection, this bizarre image made sense to the dreamer because her friend was an artist. The dream was a reminder to nurture her own creativity before it died. The rabbit—a very fertile animal— was the perfect symbol.

Day residue: TV programs, movies, books

The images from our day show up in our dreams. Many years ago, when I worked as a microbiologist, I had Petri plates in my dreams. Now I am doing yoga postures in dreams, and I do them so much better than I can in class. Only in my dreams can I touch my forehead to my toes with my legs straight and do a perfect standing bow!

Freud called this *day residue*, a spilling over into our dreaming minds of what was in our field of vision during the day. This is where the image comes from, but it is *not its meaning*. We use any image because it fits the story we want to tell, whether that seems immediately apparent or not. In fact, if you have an easy and obvious explanation of the image, you are probably missing a deeper layer of meaning that the dream offered. Your feelings about the image will help you understand why you picked it.

When I have my yoga dream, it is more than a wish to advance at yoga or visualizing improving my postures. It also tells me that I can do something I previously thought I couldn't, even if it doesn't refer directly to the yoga pose. The dream encourages me to try harder in other areas of my life.

Prompts

Choose the prompts that interest you most, and use the blank pages that follow to record your responses.

one

What was the last thing you saw (or thought about) before turning off your light to sleep?

★ How were these images captured in your dreams? (If you see a man with a gun in a TV movie, you may dream someone is pointing a gun at you.)

★ How is this an echo of something in your life? (How are you feeling threatened?)

★ Did the images open any of the other doorways? (A bicycle might make you remember your childhood bike, a bike trip you hope to take, or someone you know who is an avid biker. A bike is a solitary mode of transportation where the rider is relatively unprotected, and it has no engine. In that sense, a bicycle may be metaphor for progressing by your own efforts.)

two

How are your problems and concerns captured by a television program or news report? (If you see a chase scene, you might identify with the events—you are feeling as if you are being chased in some way.)

three

Describe a bizarre dream image in writing, then read it aloud. Listen for puns and special meanings.

My eyes are an ocean in which my dreams are reflected.

Anna M. Uhlich

Reality can destroy the
dream; why shouldn't
the dream destroy
reality?

George Moore

chapter 7

Doorway of Dream Story

Nobody was really surprised when it happened, not really, not on the subconscious level where savage things grow.

from *Carrie*, by
Stephen King

In each dream, you are telling yourself a story. This story has a personal purpose that only you know. You made up the story with its twists of plot. You chose the characters, costumes, setting, and outcome. You wrote all the lines of dialog and created the sequence of events *to tell yourself something you need to know.* All of this is true even when the dream seems totally alien and inexplicable.

In dream stories, the rules of reality do not apply. You can do anything in a dream, including behavior that would defy physics. You can do things that you would consider immoral in waking life, things that would get you arrested and outrage your grandmother. You can be any age or shape, male or female, a participant or an observer of your dream movie.

What is the dream story?

A story has a beginning, middle, and end. So do many dream stories. Seeing the story in its entirety, as a plot, can often help you understand what you are trying to tell yourself by having and remembering the dream. An example of a simple dream plot would be, *I am trying to get somewhere, but I keep running into obstacles that keep me from arriving at my destination.* Telling a dream in three sentences or less helps to collapse the dream into its main elements of beginning, middle, and end.

Dream stories reflect the way we tell the story of our lives. At some times we may see ourselves as victims of the malice of others, at the mercy of forces beyond our control. At other times we feel competent and capable, and our dreams will show that we are the agents of change. Our power resides within us.

Prompts

Choose the prompts that interest you most, and use the blank pages that follow to record your responses.

one

All dreams are current. How does your dream mirror your own state of mind on the day of the dream? (If I feel like my workplace contains mysterious elements and intrigue, I might be in the middle of a spy story in my dream.)

two

What is the start of the dream story?

three

What is the middle of the story? What plot twists or obstacles come up?

* What is the arc of the story? (Do things get better as they proceed? Or do they get worse?)
* What happens? List all the verbs in the story in the order you say them to see the changes in action.
* Who is the main character in the story? (You or someone else?)
* How is the main character changed by the events of the story?

four

How does the dream end? Does the story have a happy ending? A scary or unhappy one?

five

Does it make waking, logical sense? What new information is here? (Seemingly nonsensical dream events have their own kind of dream logic, which is revealed by all of the techniques in this book.)

six

How does the dream story affect the story of your life at the
time of the dream?

   ★ How is this story the same as the story of your whole
life? (Keep in mind that it might be telling you that you
need to tell yourself a new story!)

   ★ How is the dream telling you to see things in a new way?
(That is, to tell yourself a different story.) Write that new
viewpoint to your life circumstances. (Perhaps what you
have thought of as your curse is really a blessing in dis-
guise.)

seven

What does this story's outcome tell you about how you handle
problems in your daily life?

eight

Re-write the dream with a different ending—one that satisfies
you or feels more complete. If your dream story seems too
jumbled with many changes of scene and character, tell it as
orderly as you can. You can make up the missing parts. (Remember, you made it up to begin with!)

You control your future, your destiny. What you think about comes about. By recording your dreams and goals on paper, you set in motion the process of becoming the person you most want to be. Put your future in good hands—your own.

Mark Victor Hansen

So many of our dreams at
first seem impossible, then
they seem improbable, and
then, when we summon
the will, they soon become
inevitable.

Christopher Reeve

I was not looking for my
dreams to interpret my life,
but rather for my life to
interpret my dreams.

Susan Sontag

chapter 8

Doorway of Current Issues and Problems

A mediocre idea that generates
enthusiasm will go further than
a great idea that inspires no one.

Mary Kay Ash

We dream about the issues and problems in our lives that are of concern to us at the time of the dream. This is true for all dreams, even those about deceased relatives, events from the past, or places we haven't lived for many years. When we dream about people or events from the past, they usually represent incidents in our lives today, or certain emotions we associate with these incidents. Through our dreams, we seek resolution of our current issues.

Sometimes, when the meaning of a dream seems obscure, looking back at what we did and felt in the hours preceding the dream helps us to understand the dream's meaning. If I dream about a building in need of repair, this dream might refer to my health or my financial concerns, depending upon which one is on my mind at the time of the dream.

Our concerns can be personal, global, or both. Our daily actions and use of resources have an effect on the planet and its future. Our ecological concerns might express both individual and community issues. A dream of finding forgotten kittens in a closet might highlight the part of me that I need to nurture and have ignored. This same dream might simultaneously be about my worries about pet overpopulation, the endangered animals of the world, or those parts of me and/or others that need to "come out of the closet."

Prompts

Choose the prompts that interest you most, and use the blank pages that follow to record your responses.

one

What are your most pressing current concerns/problems/issues? Make a list. When making your list, be sure to consider all areas of your life: family, children, lovers, work, mental and physical health, spiritual concerns, ethical dilemmas, creative outlets, authenticity, etc.

★ How does your dream highlight these concerns?

two

What was the last thing you were thinking about before you went to sleep?

three

What are you worried about lately? What is your biggest worry?

four

What new and helpful information does your dream offer about these concerns? Does the dream indicate an alternate path or an action that you haven't considered before? Is it viable?

five

What plans are you making (professional, financial, vacation, relocating, moving)?

six

What needs to be addressed in your relationship(s)?

seven

What have you been holding in?

eight

What do you need to say aloud?

nine

What are you most looking forward to?

ten

What are you feeling optimistic about?

98 | If one advances confidently
in the direction of his
dreams and endeavors to
lead a life which he has
imagined, he will meet with
a success unexpected in
common hours.

Henry David Thoreau

100 | Dream is not a
revelation....
Dream—a scintillating
mirage surrounded by
shadows—is essentially
poetry.

Michel Leiris

102 | I have spread my dreams
under your feet. Tread
softly because you tread
on my dreams.

W.B. Yeats

chapter 9

Doorway of Memory

The difference between false
memories and true ones is the same
as for jewels: it is always the false
ones that look the most real,
the most brilliant.

Salvador Dali

Dreams and memories are not the same. Many people believe that dreams are a doorway to memory, or that dreams are a special kind of memory. This is untrue, and has led to some disturbing outcomes for people who attempt to "recover memories" through their dreams. When examining memories through your dreams, be careful about jumping to conclusions about events.

The emotions and images in dreams may remind us of events we've forgotten, earlier states of mind and feelings. Dreams can call up an existing memory that we recognize, but they do not uncover previously "repressed" memories. These old images may just be reminders of similar feelings in our present lives.

Sometimes a dream will be a review of an event that happened that still haunts us. I may dream of my parents because I still have issues with them and things I never got to say—though they have both been dead for many years. The dream brings up these old feelings associated with my past events to remind me that some similar feeling has come up in my present, waking circumstances—perhaps with someone who reminds me of one of my parents.

Common examples are being in your childhood home in a dream, driving a car you no longer own, being with friends you haven't seen in many years, finding yourself with an ex-lover, or working at a former job. These memories or nostalgic contexts may be a doorway to meaning.

Prompts

Choose the prompts that interest you most, and use the blank pages that follow to record your responses.

one

What memory is triggered by your dream? (A particular lamp might make me think of the antiques in my aunt's home, and that will lead to questions about my aunt and her character as it relates to mine.)

two

What associations are related to the memory? (Memories can have strings of associations—to other people, places, and what they represent for you.)

three

How are your current circumstances mirroring the remembered emotions, events, places, or persons?

four

Who in your life now is acting like this person from the past?

five

What lesson was in the remembered event that applies in the present?

six

Are you repeating an old pattern that needs to be changed?

Keep some souvenirs of
your past, or how will you
ever prove it wasn't all a
dream?

Ashleigh Brilliant

110 | All the things one has
forgotten scream for
help in dreams.

Elias Canetti

chapter 10

Doorway of Dream Objects and Symbols

Art can only be truly Art by
presenting an adequate outward
symbol of some fact in the
interior life.

Margaret Fuller

Anything in a dream can be a symbol, including places, people, animals, and things.

Certain objects carry an emotional charge in our dreams, just as they do in waking life. Commonly, guns and knives are fearful objects in our daily lives, but we may not feel the same way about them in a dream. Or we may feel fear about something else in our lives, but we focus on the *knife* rather than on the *person* who is "cutting us up" in a metaphorical sense. Someone might be "shooting us down" with emotional put-downs, and so the gun represents this hostility. Any object can have meaning beyond the obvious interpretations.

Some symbols in dreams seem very odd or offend our waking consciousness. Toilet dreams and bodily excretions fall into this category, as well as very explicit sexual imagery or violence. It is hard to get past our emotional reaction to a symbol we find repulsive, but with patience, we discover how appropriate the symbol was. A dream of piles of human feces might be one you would prefer not to examine! However, it might be offering you the important message that you are getting buried in a bunch of crap in your waking life—someone else's nonsensical ideas or too many unnecessary material belongings.

Sometimes, the juxtaposition of objects seems odd. A classic example would be seeing an adult in a dream dressed in baby clothing or diapers. The dreamer is making a clear evaluation of this person's immaturity, but on waking, the dreamer must decide what relevance this judgement has in her life.

Remember, all symbols have personal, private meanings. The same symbol, when it occurs in two people's dreams, could have two very different interpretations. Building your own "dream dictionary" (see page 16) can help you discover what your recurring symbols mean to you.

Prompts

Choose the prompts that interest you most, and use the blank pages that follow to record your responses.

one

What objects are in your dream? Make a list of the objects (house, car, chair, etc.) in your dream.

two

What objects appear regularly in your dreams? (Computers? Cars? Furniture? Kitchen gadgets? Clocks? Work tools?)

* ✶ What are your feelings about and associations to these objects?
* ✶ Think about these objects and how they might relate to your life. How are your current circumstances symbolized by these objects?

three

Think of an incongruous object that appeared in your dream. What does this tell you? (I dreamed about eating old photographs that belonged to a friend, and then felt guilty. This dream was about my concerns about using real memories in writing a novel.)

four

How do the objects in your dreams represent parts of you? (Try to answer this even if the objects seem offensive, repulsive, or weird.)

five

Write an imaginary dialog with the object and ask it to reveal its message.

* ✶ If the object is unrecognizable, what are your feelings toward it? What might it be?
* ✶ List possible uses.
* ✶ What does it remind you of?

★ How does the description of your feelings toward the object sound like your feelings about something else in your life?

★ Draw the object. What does it look like or remind you of?

★ Shape or sculpt the object in clay or papier-mâché.

six

Write down your most frequently used symbols and begin to compile your own *personal* dream dictionary.

Dreams are illustrations
from the book your soul is
writing about you.

Marsha Norman

It is in our idleness, in our
dreams, that the submerged
truth sometimes comes to
the top.

Virginia Woolf

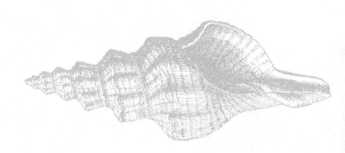

I feel very adventurous.
There are so many doors to
be opened, and I'm not
afraid to look behind them.

Elizabeth Taylor

chapter 11

Doorway of Nightmares and Repeating Dream Themes

Have you ever noticed there is never any third act to a nightmare? They bring you to a climax of terror and then leave you there.

Max Beerbohm

One of the most distressing experiences of dreaming is the nightmare. Even worse is the recurring nightmare. Usually, the dreamer will wake in terror—with a pounding heart, a sweat-drenched body, and a real fear of danger in the room. Depending on the person and the content of the dream, these very uncomfortable feelings might linger for a minute or for several days. Commonly, a person will wake from a nightmare and feel distressed for several hours, affecting work, relationships, etc. This can be true even for people who are able to clearly differentiate that this was "only a dream" and not real in any way. Recurring nightmares can interfere with ordinary coping skills.

Most people don't want to hear that nightmares are very helpful and valuable. They don't want to have these dreams at all! And they'd rather not analyze them. The last thing they want to do is to focus on their nightmares and discover the meanings under the surface.

But for the nightmares to stop, you have to understand the message they are trying to convey. If you have chosen such a distressing method of telling this story to yourself, you have a good reason. The dream is showing you how distressed you already are and how much you need to change something in your life. Doing dreamwork through any of the doorways we've discussed will help you understand the content and message of your nightmare. The writing prompts below are for recurrent dreams and nightmares in particular.

Prompts

Choose the prompts that interest you most, and use the blank pages that follow to record your responses.

one

Notice the timing of your nightmare. What events preceded this dream?

two

What makes it a nightmare for you?

three

What are the strongest emotions in the dream? (Mortal terror or fear of death is the most commonly cited example of nightmarish emotion.) List three emotions that are part of your most common nightmares.

★ What in your life feels "nightmarish" in the same way? (Note that the dream is an *exaggeration* of these feelings to get your attention.)

★ How is this particular dream, in all its dreadful imagery, telling you about your true feelings toward something in your life?

★ What have you neglected or ignored in your life? What do you need to change or revise? (This question can be asked at any time, even if you're not having nightmares.)

four

When did the recurring dream or nightmare begin? (This is a big clue to meaning. The first occurrence of a recurring nightmare might be after the death of a family member or some other traumatic event.)

five

If you no longer have this nightmare, when did it stop? (You may have made a life change that addressed the issues raised by the nightmare without realizing it.)

six

What is the nightmare telling you that you need to *do*?

seven

What change is it time to make in your life *now*?

Dreams say what they
mean, but they don't say
it in daytime language.

Gail Godwin

If you want your dreams
to come true, don't
oversleep.

Yiddish Proverb

Teachers open the door, but
you must enter by yourself.

Chinese Proverb

chapter 12

Doorway of Dream Connections

The man who has begun to live more
seriously within begins to live more
simply without.

Ernest Hemingway

Every dream is about the issues in your life at the time of the dream. Even when you dream of people and places long gone from your present life, these images have relevance today—or you would not have chosen them to use in your current dream.

When thinking about a dream, we will automatically make connections or have associations to people, places, and predicaments. These connections can lead us to any of the doorways discussed previously. Or, using the suggestions for one of those doorways might lead us to an association. Associations are the mental connections we make to previous experiences, emotions, and people, to our beliefs, and to familiar concepts.

We make connections and associations automatically. New people remind us of those we knew in the past. New ideas are processed by comparing them with what we already know and with past experiences. This is how we begin to understand anything new. Making connections helps us to understand dreams, too.

For example, you might see a big soup pot in your dream, and that might take you to a memory of your grandmother's kitchen and her vegetable soup. You might think of the emphasis on food and food preparation while you were growing up, and the meanings attributed to food. This opens the doorways of memory and image, leading you to the doorways of feelings and current concerns. These are all ways to examine and understand your dreams.

Remember that all the doorways are part of the same structure. Entering the dream through any of the doorways will make the others more comprehensible to you.

Prompts

Choose the prompts that interest you most, and use the blank pages that follow to record your responses.

one

Write a detailed description of your most recent dream.

two

What connections do you make spontaneously as you write about the dream or tell it aloud?

three

What past events come into awareness on reviewing this dream?

four

What issues, people, and emotions come up as you write or tell this dream?

five

What connections do you make between the feelings in the dream and the feelings in your daily life?

six

Think about the hidden or deeper meanings of these connections. What do they tell you about your present waking life?

seven

How do the dream's metaphors connect with your most pressing issues (feeling stuck, paralyzed, held back, obstructed, high, or soaring)?

eight

What does the dream place in the foreground by the strength of its vivid images and emotions? That is, what is most important in your psychological and emotional life now?

The dream ego knows
things during the dream
that the waking ego
doesn't know.

D. Patrick Miller

138 | Dreams pass into the reality
of action. From the action
stems the dream again;
and this interdependence
produces the highest form
of living.

Anaïs Nin

chapter 13

Doorway of Dream Messages

First thoughts have tremendous
energy. The internal censor usually
squelches them, so we live in the realm
of second and third thoughts, thoughts
on thought, twice and three times
removed from the direct connection
of the first fresh flash.

Natalie Goldberg

We say children's stories have a *moral* or a *teaching*. Many dreams
offer a moral or maxim in the same way—we say the dream offers an *insight*. It is what a good therapist will help you to see
when you do dreamwork in counseling. It is new information—a new perspective, a whole different angle.

Sometimes our dreams ask us to see our situation differently. When we do, we can react accordingly and change our
emotions toward people and events. Our changes in behavior
result in others changing how they respond to and interact
with us.

If you are likely to make excuses and rationalize your
problems, your dreams will let you know. They will tell you that
you are denying you have a problem, your contribution to the

problem, or how you make it worse. Waking denials include, "I never get angry," "I can quit" (from someone with a gambling, drug, or alcohol addiction), or "I can handle this" (when it's clear you need some kind of professional help).

Giving titles to your dreams

When you give your dream a title, you capture the message of the dream in just a few words. This helps you understand it, too. Looking at a list of titles, you will see your personal evolution. A list of titles might demonstrate when you are concerned mostly with fear and anxiety in your dreams, or how you might often see yourself in competition with others. Another person might be focused on power and control and use a variety of dream metaphors to express this, including prestige, sex, wealth, and knowledge.

Choose a title that will help to trigger the memory of that particular dream, rather than something generic and non-specific. "Diving happily into a pool of blood" is a more vivid title than "Diving" or "Swimming." You will become more adept at finding the most fitting title for a dream as you record dreams daily. A good title captures the essence of a dream, along with the emotions it evoked for the dreamer.

Prompts

Choose the prompts that interest you most, and use the blank pages that follow to record your responses.

one

What are you trying to tell yourself with this dream? (Another character in the dream might seem to hold this wisdom.)

two

What is the maxim or moral of your dream?

Three examples:

A. *If you keep doing what you're doing, you'll stay stuck and paralyzed.*

B. *The way you're behaving is the same as jumping off a cliff.*

C. *You're hiding from the problem. Get out and face your dragons.*

three

Translate your dream message into a message or action plan for your life.

For the three messages above:

A. *Your job makes you feel stuck and powerless; look for another.*

B. *Rushing into marriage with someone you don't know is the equivalent of jumping off a cliff. Look before you leap!*

C. *Instead of hiding, face your problems and see what you can do about them.*

four

What solutions to the problem are in your dream?

five

What new information does the dream offer?

six

What insight is in your dream? What does it tell you about yourself that you didn't know before?

seven

How does the dream dispute or address your waking denial or procrastination?

eight

Nightmares and recurrent dreams are gifts. We emphasize these important messages by repeating them or making them so striking and so emotional that they wake us up. What are your nightmares and recurrent dreams trying to tell you?

nine

Does the title you gave your dream reveal some message you've missed?

ten

Make a list of your dream titles and write about any pattern you observe. You might want to keep an ongoing list of titles as you create them, or you can go back and make a list from earlier dreams you've recorded in your dream journal.

144 | Dreams the sources of
action, the meeting and
the end, a resting-place
among the flight of
things.

Muriel Rukeyser

.

There is no easy method of learning difficult things. The method is to close the door, give out that you are not at home, and work.

Joseph Marie De Maistre

chapter 14

Taking Action on Your Dream Message

We need to dream big dreams, propose
grandiose means if we are to recapture
the excitement, the vibrancy, and pride
we once had.

Coleman Young

Stepping through dream doorways is more than just understanding
the content of a dream or why you had it. It's about using the
information the dream offers to have a better life, to use your
talents and gifts fully. Too often, people do some kind of inner
work through a spiritual discipline or in psychotherapy and
come away saying, "Oh, yes. I have a problem with working
with others [or with authority]. I know that." So, if you *know*
about that defect of character, what are you going to *do* about
it? Do you want to change? Do you want to continue to suffer
or struggle? Or have you just found a better excuse for your
past behavior?

Dreams call for us to be more reflective in our lives. They
tell us when we are being irresponsible to ourselves and others. They tell us we can grow, be more whole, and have our
lives in better balance. But having this wisdom and not acting
on it defeats the effort expended in doing dreamwork.

Thoughts, feelings, behavior

We can take the message of the dream into action by making a change in our thoughts, feelings, and/or behavior. Your dream might suggest making a change in one or more of these areas. Making a change in your thinking will affect how you feel and behave. Similarly, changing any one of these areas affects the other two. Having one core area of personal improvement seems to have a ripple effect into other areas of your life.

Asking for a new dream

If you're still uncertain about your dream's meanings or what you should do with the information you have learned from the dream, you can ask your "dream machine" to give you more help. When you go to bed at night, ask for another dream with metaphors that you can understand! Ask for assistance or more information to make a decision (an action) the dream seems to call for. You may want to do this in your dream journal or simply go to bed with a question in mind. You can even write the question on a small slip of paper and carry it in your pocket during the day. Each time you feel the slip of paper in your pocket, you will be reminding your unconscious that you are asking for more help.

Prompts

Choose the prompts that interest you most, and use the blank pages that follow to record your responses.

one

Which action is most clear in the dream? Are you thinking? Feeling (emotional reactions)? Or doing (behaving)? Do your actions in any of these three areas (or all of them) need to change?

* What new perspective or thinking does the dream suggest?
* How are your feelings or emotions changed by this dream?
* What does the dream tell you to *do* differently?
* Are you doing something in the dream that you thought you couldn't do? If yes, what is the dream telling you that you can do—either literally or metaphorically?
* If the dream is a message from your higher self, what is it asking you to do now?

two

Sometimes I fly in my dreams (without a plane). I know I can't fly literally, but this is always a dream to tell me how well I'm doing. I take it as encouragement to go to the next level of my abilities. In what way are *you* ready to fly?

three

Write out the question you want your dream to answer. (Blurt it out!) It may come out something like: "I don't get it. What am I supposed to do? Tell me again so I can understand." Use words that you would speak most naturally.

* If the dream you get in response is still obscure, perhaps you've been too tentative or gentle in your question. Try again with a more direct approach. Don't be polite. Make sure your question can be answered with an essay instead of a yes-or-no answer. Write that more direct question down.

* Another variation: "Okay, dear dream machine, I hear you talking, but you're not speaking my language. Give it to me more simply this time, in words I can understand. Draw me a picture." Reword this request in your own way.

* "Dream Maker, the messages you send confuse and upset me; tell me in a way that I can hear you!" Reword to suit your confusion or lack of understanding.

four –

If you're still stumped, ask a trusted friend to listen to your dream and then comment on it by beginning, "If it were my dream...." Write down what he or she says.

152 Myths are public dreams,
dreams are private myths.

Joseph Campbell

154 Every challenge we face
can be solved by a
dream.

David Schwartz

chapter 15

Further Incubations

To think is to differ.

Clarence Darrow

I don't make New Year's resolutions, but I do set goals—usually around the New Year and whenever else I want to reconsider some aspect of my life.

Often, a dream will come to address the goals and visions we have for the future—to encourage, clarify, or caution us on our life paths. We can ask for this kind of guidance without waiting for our dreams to offer it by incubating a dream question.

You may want to ask yourself any of the following questions before going to bed. Expect an answer. Examine the dream you have in response to the question.

When you "incubate" or program these questions in anticipation of an answer in a dream, know that you will get the answer you *most need to hear*. Your dream may seem unrelated to your question, but approach it as a helpful answer in metaphorical language. Make up your own questions as they occur to you and keep a list of them.

1. What is my mission?
2. What do I need to know about myself that is out of my awareness?
3. What is my purpose? (Dream Weaver, please send me a sign!)
4. What lessons can I learn from my present situation (struggles, problems)?
5. What am I doing wrong concerning _____?
6. How can I be more successful at _____?
7. Show me my true self.
8. How can I be an agent of peace and harmony in my_____
   (workplace, home, family, organization, etc.)?
9. Who is my mirror?
10. Shine a light on my blind spots.
11. What will satisfy my longing?
12. I wish _____

    _____

13. Show me how to make this wish a reality.
14. Show me my bliss.
15. How can I manifest my bliss?
16. How can I be more at peace with myself?
17. Show me my truth.
18. What do I need to know today?
19. What baggage do I need to shed?
20. How can I overcome the obstacles I see ahead of me?
21. Dream Weaver, I need encouragement. Send me some good dreams to support what I am doing today. (Be specific about what you want to accomplish.)
22. Make up a list of questions and requests about your life concerns that you can return to periodically, such as at the start of each New Year.
23. Add any of your own incubations here:_____

    _____

Conclusion

The best way to make your dreams
come true is to wake up.

Paul Valery

Your dream journal is a tool for you to better understand yourself and what you need to do to live the best life you can have—including good health, satisfying work, loving relationships, and an opportunity to be all that you are. You can choose the techniques and doorways that best suit your style of personal exploration and discovery.

Your dream journal can prepare you for a dream partner or a dream group that will spread to others the benefits you have come to appreciate in following your dreams.

Enjoy your dream journal, and take pleasure in the comfort it offers you every day.

It may be those who do most, dream most.

Stephen Leacock

Bibliography

Adams, Kathleen. 1990. *Journal to the Self: Twenty-Two Paths to Personal Growth.* Warner Books.

Alvarez, A. 1995. *Night: Night Life, Night Language Sleep, and Dreams.* W.W. Norton.

Cameron, Julia. 1992. *The Artist's Way.* Jeremy P. Tarcher.

Capacchione, Lucia. 1979. *The Creative Journal.* Newcastle.

Delaney, Gayle. 1991. *Breakthrough Dreaming.* Bantam Books.

Epel, Naomi (ed). 1993. *Writers Dreaming.* Carol Southern Books.

Faraday, Ann. 1972. *Dream Power.* Berkley Medallion.

———. 1974. *The Dream Game.* Perennial / Harper & Row.

Fox, John. 1995. *Finding What You Didn't Lose: Expressing Your Truth and Creativity Through Poem-Making.* Jeremy P. Tarcher.

———. 1997. *Poetic Medicine: The Healing Art of Poem-Making.* Jeremy P. Tarcher.

Gackenbach, Jayne (ed). 1991. *Dream Images: A Call to Mental Arms.* Baywood Publishing.

Garfield, Patricia. 1974. *Creative Dreaming.* Ballantine.

Gendlin, Eugene T. 1986. *Let Your Body Interpret Your Dreams.* Chiron Publications.

Goldberg, Natalie. 1986. *Writing Down the Bones.* Shambhala.

Harary, K. & Weintraub, P. 1989. *Lucid Dreams in 30 Days.* St. Martin's Press.

Harman, W. & Rheingold, H. 1984. *Higher Creativity.* Jeremy P. Tarcher, Inc.

Johnson, Robert A. 1986. *Inner Work.* HarperSanFrancisco.

———. 1991. *Owning Your Own Shadow: Understanding the Dark Side of the Psyche.* HarperSanFrancisco.

Krakow, Barry, & Neidhardt, J. 1992. *Conquering Bad Dreams & Nightmares.* Berkley Books.

Krippner, Stanley. 1990. *Dreamtime & Dreamwork.* Jeremy P. Tarcher, Inc.

LaBerge, S. & Rheingold H. 1990. *Exploring the World of Lucid Dreaming.* Ballantine Books.

LaBerge, Stephen. 1985. *Lucid Dreaming.* Ballantine Books.

Loftus, E. & Ketchum, K. 1994. *The Myth of Repressed Memory.* St. Martin's Griffin.

Maisel, Eric. 1995. *Fearless Creating.* Jeremy P. Tarcher.

———. 1999. *Deep Writing.* Jeremy P. Tarcher.

Mazza, Joan. 1998. *Dreaming Your Real Self: A Personal Ap-

160

proach to Dream Interpretation. Perigee.

Mazza, Joan. 2000. *Dream Back Your Life: Transforming Dream Messages Into Life Action—A Practical Guide to Dreams, Daydreams, and Fantasies*. Perigee.

Moore, Thomas. 1992. *Care of the Soul: A Guide for Cultivating Depth and Sacredness in Everyday Life*. HarperCollins.

Morris, Jill. 1985. *The Dream Workbook*. Fawcett Crest.

Moss, Robert. 1996. *Conscious Dreaming*. Crown.

Palmer, Helen (ed.). 1998. *Inner Knowing: Consciousness, Creativity, Insight, Intuition*. Jeremy P. Tarcher/Putnam.

Perry, Susan K. 1999. *Writing in Flow: Keys to Enhanced Creativity*. Writer's Digest Books.

———. 1990. *Playing Smart*. Free Spirit Pub.

Rainer, Tristine. 1978. *The New Diary*. Jeremy P. Tarcher, Inc.

Siegel, Alan. 1990. *Dreams That Can Change Your Life*. Berkley.

Siegel, Alan, and Bulkeley, Kelly. 1998. *Dreamcatching: Every Parent's Guide to Exploring and Understanding Children's Dreams and Nightmares*. Three Rivers Press.

Simon, Sidney B. 1988. *Getting Unstuck: Breaking Through Your Barriers to Change*. Warner Books.

Tavris, Carol. 1989. *Anger: The Misunderstood Emotion*. Touchstone.

Taylor, Jeremy. 1992. *Where People Fly and Water Runs Uphill*. Warner Books.

———. 1998. *The Living Labyrinth: Exploring Universal Themes in Myths, Dreams, and the Symbolism of Waking Life*. Paulist Press.

Taylor, Jeremy.1983. *Dreamwork*. Paulist Press.

Ullman, Montague, & Zimmerman, N. 1979. *Working With Dreams*. Jeremy P. Tarcher.

Walsh, Roger N., and Vaughan, Frances (eds.). 1993. *Paths Beyond Ego: The Transpersonal Vision*. Jeremy P. Tarcher.

Whitmont, Edward. & Perera, S. 1989. *Dreams, A Portal to the Source*. Routledge Press.

Zweig, Connie, and Abrams, Jeremiah, editors. 1991. *Meeting the Shadow: The Hidden Power of the Dark Side of Human Nature*. Jeremy P. Tarcher.

Zweig, Connie, and Wolf, Steve. 1997. *Romancing the Shadow: Illuminating the Dark Side of the Soul*. Ballantine.